Vision 2025 - the Startup Forecast

The Grumpy Entrepreneur and David Murray-Hundley

Published by The Grumpy Entrepreneur, 2023.

While every precaution has been taken in the preparation of this book, the publisher assumes no responsibility for errors or omissions, or for damages resulting from the use of the information contained herein.

VISION 2025 - THE STARTUP FORECAST

First edition. May 15, 2023.

ISBN: 979-8223338123

Written by The Grumpy Entrepreneur and David Murray-Hundley.

Of course dedicated to my Trina, Harriet and Georgie

My first boss happened to be a startup inside a bank called Chase - Kevin Doyle. His years of putting up with me have been a challenge for him.

And to Gordon Ramsey's dad, who ran newsagents in Bradley arcade, Bretch Hill, Banbury and where I purchased Computer Shopper to use as content for my CV into my first startup.

Vision 2025 - The Startup Forecast

"Never do startups just because of the money, do it to make a difference" DMH

Introduction

I have spent a lot of time around startups, most of it good, some of that time not so good and some of the very small moments appalling. In fact I have spent almost 30 years doing or around startups. In fact when I did my first one, or at least attempted to with a friend you still went to bank managers with a full plan (a loan that got approved by the way) and match funded with the duke of edinburgh fund. Anyway lucky for us we were tougher on our plan than the bank as it turns out and didn't move it forward.

I then got to work on early web companies when the rest of the world was busy watching Friends and saying "I will never need an email address" and what Compuserve is.

By the time the Dotcom Boom arrived, I had worked for 3 startups here in the UK and in the US.

Dotcom saw me as part of a DoTcom darling, Commerce One based in Silicon Valley. We IPO'd on NASDAQ in 1999 and hit $22bn market cap and had only made profit 1 quarter. This is experience is a whole different book. But a time that won't happen again and I loved the roller coaster. And the book would be more like "The Wolf of Wall Street" but without the drugs, well in my case anyway.

Then even after the bubble burst I was still out there helping recover startups that had no more cash or just waited for the next wave to happen.

Oh and I went bankrupt and it was one of the best things that happened to me

In recent years, I must have spoken to 1000s of startup founders, x10 about the amount of decks I have seen and invested in a few of them. Even had a few exits and seen a few have plenty of challenges.

Since 2012 you just have to look at linkedin to see how many people have startups, call themselves entrepreneurs etc. It's the noisiest I have ever seen it.

As my good friend Kevin Doyles says "you cannot call yourself an Entrepreneur until you have actually got a return for your investors". It's very true.

So why did I put this book together?

One of the things I have found on my journey is that it's very hard to know what's around the corner but you do get older, more experienced and can see more trends about to happen. You don't always get it right, but you definitely get better. You won't believe how many founders I meet and I can tell pretty much what will happen with them for the next 12 or 24 months.

I also wrote this book to inspire 1 person who has never done a startup and wants to but is starting with zero idea. You can be 18 or 60 it doesn't matter but it's always good to help.

I wrote this book to inspire a current founder not to worry about the future.

I wrote this book to see if I get it right, we will soon know.

I wrote this book to inspire me to do more.

This whole journey for me started at the age of 18 sleeping in a bus shelter in Milton Keynes, but again thats a different book. However sometimes we need to find motivation to do things.

So I have done my job if one person gets something positive, some motivation at maybe a not so great time. Emjoy David Murray-Hundley "The Grumpy Entrepreneur"

1 Ecosystem of Startups

1.1. Understanding the Startup Ecosystem

LISTEN UP, KIDDOS. Sit down, grab a kale smoothie, or whatever it is you're drinking these days, because it's time for a crash course in the wonderfully convoluted world of startups. Brace yourself, it's about as straightforward as a hedge maze... at night... during a fog... with one eye closed.

First, we have the startup founders, the heroes of our tale (or villains, depending on how many times they pivot their business model). They're easy to spot - just look for the bleary-eyed individuals hunched over laptops, muttering about scalable solutions, disruptive technologies, and market penetration. They love their buzzwords, don't they? And if they're not talking about their revolutionary app idea, they're probably pitching it to their barista, Uber driver, or anyone unfortunate enough to be within earshot.

Then we've got the venture capitalists, or VCs. Picture sharks in expensive suits, circling the waters for the scent of the next 'unicorn'. They're the ones with the money, honey, and they're not afraid to use it. But beware, their funds often come with more strings attached than a marionette.

Ah, angel investors, the fairy godparents of the startup world. They swoop in with their magic wands (read: checkbooks), ready to turn your pumpkin of an idea into a shiny, new startup carriage. With a flick of their wrist (or more accurately, a wire transfer), they're ready to make your entrepreneurial dreams come true.

But let's be clear, angel investors aren't all halo and wings. They're shrewd businesspeople, often with a portfolio as diverse as a hipster's record collection. They're looking for the next big thing, a unicorn among a stable full of donkeys. They can spot a weak business model from a mile off and are as likely to scrutinize your financial projections as a food critic analyzing a seven-course tasting menu.

So, while they might descend from the heavens with a golden parachute of funding, remember, they're not just investing in your idea, they're investing in you. It's like a marriage, but with term sheets and equity stakes. So, make sure you're ready to say 'I do' before you walk down the startup aisle. After all, as any seasoned entrepreneur knows, with great capital comes great responsibility... and an investor or two ready to hold your feet to the fire.

Next up, the hustling freelancers - the jacks-of-all-trades, masters of none. They're the Swiss Army knives of the startup world, with a tool for every job and a caffeine addiction that would make a barista shudder. Always on the move, they flit from one gig to the next, spreading ideas like pollen on a windy day.

Can't forget the tech bros, can we? They roam the ecosystem in packs, armed with a vocabulary that sounds more like a secret code than business talk. If they're not in a heated debate about the merits of Python over Ruby, they're planning the launch of the next 'Uber for something-that-doesn't-need-an-Uber'.

Oh, the exhilarating chatter of exits and IPOs. It's all everyone in the startup ecosystem can seem to gab on about, like a flock of overexcited parakeets after a double espresso. I swear, you can't swing a cat in a WeWork without hitting some bright-eyed founder dreaming of ringing the bell at the NYSE.

Now, don't get me wrong, I'm all for a good exit strategy. It's like knowing where the fire escapes are in a crowded theater. Essential, but not why you bought the ticket. You're there for the show, the thrill of the performance, the drama of the plot twists. Likewise, in the world of startups, it's about the journey, the hustle, the thrill of turning an idea scribbled on a beer mat into a functioning business.

But these days, everyone's got 'IPO' on the brain. It's as if the moment you start a company, you're supposed to be plotting your path to Wall Street. Because, you know, nothing says 'I've made it' like subjecting yourself to the merciless scrutiny of public shareholders, navigating a maze of regulatory filings, and regularly waking up in a cold sweat at the thought of quarterly earnings calls.

Remember, folks, an IPO is not the be-all and end-all. It's just one potential pit stop on the wild ride that is running a startup. So, let's focus less on the exit sign and more on the road ahead, shall we? After all, the journey is half the fun. And by 'fun', I mean a rollercoaster ride of sleepless nights, caffeine overdoses, and relentless problem-solving. Ah, the startup life. You've got to love it. Or at least, be slightly masochistic.

Finally, there's the elusive bootstrapped startup. As rare as a well-done steak at a vegan convention, these startups shun the glitz and glamour of VC funding, choosing instead to burn the midnight oil and subsist on a diet of instant ramen and cheap coffee. They're the underdogs, the dreamers, the ones who make you want to root for them, even when their business plan looks like it was written on a cocktail napkin.

In this mad, mad world of startups, it's not the strongest or the fastest that survive, but the ones most responsive to change. And by change, I mean the ability to morph your artisanal cheese app into a blockchain for hamsters when the market demands it.

So, welcome to the startup ecosystem, my friends. It's a wild ride, full of ups, downs, and enough jargon to fill a dictionary. But hey, who said entrepreneurship was supposed to be easy?

1.2. The Role of Startups in the Global Economy

WELL, WELL, WELL. NOW that we've gotten a rough idea of what the startup ecosystem looks like, let's delve into the role these caffeine-fueled, buzzword-spewing entities play in the global economy. Prepare for a wild ride, folks. This journey has more ups and downs than a rollercoaster during an earthquake.

You see, startups are a lot like popcorn. Stick with me here, I promise this will make sense. You throw a bunch of kernels (startups) into a hot pot (the market), and you wait. Some of them pop and turn into something delicious (successful businesses), filling the air with a tantalizing aroma (economic growth). Others, well, they just sit at the bottom, burning and turning into little black nuggets of disappointment (failed ventures).

But let's not focus on the failures, shall we? It's too early in the day for that level of cynicism, even for me. Instead, let's talk about the popcorn that pops.

Startups, like our successfully popped kernels, are major drivers of innovation. They're the ones who look at the way we've been doing things for years and say, "Nah, let's do it differently." They're the ones willing to take risks, to fail, to pivot, and to occasionally create something that completely changes the game. Think about companies like Uber, Airbnb, or SpaceX. They all started as tiny kernels in the pot of the global economy.

But it's not just about disrupting industries and making boatloads of cash. No, startups also play a significant role in job creation. And I'm not just talking about jobs for software developers and digital marketing gurus. I'm talking about jobs across the board. After all, every successful startup needs a team to keep things running, from finance and legal to HR and customer service. And let's not forget the ripple effect successful startups have on their local economies. More jobs mean more disposable income, which leads to increased spending, which benefits other businesses in the area.

On the flip side, when startups fail, they can leave a crater-sized hole in the economy. Employees lose their jobs, investors lose their money, and the local economy can take a hit. But even in failure, startups contribute to the economic cycle. They create space for new ideas to flourish, and the lessons learned from their failures can help future entrepreneurs avoid the same pitfalls.

So there you have it, the role of startups in the global economy. It's a high-stakes game of risk and reward, success and failure, popping corn and burning kernels. But hey, isn't that what makes it all so exciting? Now, if you'll excuse me, all this talk of popcorn has made me hungry.

1.3. Challenges of the Past: A Look Back at Startup Trends

ALRIGHT, SETTLE DOWN. It's time for a little history lesson. Don't worry, I'll make it as painless as possible. You might even crack a smile or two. We're going on a journey through the time, revisiting the ghosts of startups past. Buckle up, because it's going to be a bumpy ride.

Back in the day - and by 'the day,' I mean the dot-com bubble of the late '90s and early 2000s - everyone and their grandmother wanted to start an internet company. Slap ".com" at the end of a noun, pitch a half-baked business plan, and voila! You were a millionaire on paper. Never mind that your company didn't actually turn a profit, or that your business model made as much sense as a fish riding a bicycle. You were "on the internet," and that was enough. Until it wasn't, and the bubble burst, leaving a trail of failed startups in its wake.

On the success side, we had the likes of Amazon and eBay. They were the cool kids at the dotcom party. They managed to turn their fledgling online platforms into global powerhouses. Amazon, with its 'sell everything, including the kitchen sink' approach, and eBay, turning your trash into someone else's treasure. They were the survivors of the dotcom wild ride, the ones who walked out of the casino with their pockets full.

But let's not forget the failures, the spectacular flameouts. Who could forget Pets.com with its sock puppet mascot and a burn rate that would make even the most reckless spender blush? Or Webvan, the grocery delivery service that built more infrastructure than a small country before realizing that maybe, just maybe, they should focus on making some money. It was like watching a slow-motion car crash, but with more schadenfreude.

The dotcom boom was a masterclass in irrational exuberance, a cautionary tale for the startup world. But as any grumpy entrepreneur will tell you, you've got to learn from the past to avoid making the same mistakes in the future. Or at least make new, more exciting mistakes. Because in the world of startups, failure is just success running a little late.

And to finish on the dotcom boom and show how crazy it was a time filled with as many PR stunts as there were IPOs. One that takes the cake, or rather the crust, has to be the infamous million-dollar pixel stunt by Pixelotto.

This hare-brained scheme was concocted by a 21-year-old Brit named Alex Tew. The idea was simple, yet utterly absurd. He set up a website with a million pixels and sold each pixel for a dollar. The buyers, mostly dotcom businesses, could use these pixels to display an image or logo, which would link back to their own site. It was like a digital billboard, but with the charm of a patchwork quilt made by a drunk spider.

And the craziest part? It worked. The site became a viral sensation. Companies were tripping over themselves to buy a piece of this pixelated pie, and in less than six months, Tew had sold out. He made a cool million dollars, all from a website that looked like a 90s screensaver.

Now, I'm not saying we should all start selling pixels. But this story is a reminder that in the wild and wacky world of startups, sometimes the craziest ideas are the ones that pay off. But remember, for every successful pixel-selling venture, there's a dozen others that crashed and burned. So, tread carefully, my entrepreneurial friends. And keep those PR stunts within the realm of sanity, or at least legality.

Then came the social media boom. If your startup didn't have a social element, you might as well have been selling fax machines. Everyone wanted to be the next Facebook or Twitter, and for a while, it seemed like every other startup was trying to make 'fetch' happen with some new social platform. But as we now know, most of these platforms had the lifespan of a fruit fly. It was a time everyone chassed after the hype companies. Even the big boys and girls can get it wrong.

Take Google+, for example. A social networking platform launched by the tech giant to rival Facebook. They had the resources, the technical expertise, and the user base. What could possibly go wrong? Well, as it turns out, a lot. Users found it confusing and unnecessary. Google tried to force it down people's throats by linking it to other Google services, resulting in a backlash rather than engagement. Ultimately, Google+ went the way of the dodo, serving as a stark reminder that even the big players can fumble the social media ball.

Or how about Ello? The ad-free, invite-only social network that was touted as the "Facebook killer". It burst onto the scene in 2014 with promises of a user-friendly, privacy-focused platform. The hype was real. But alas, it couldn't deliver on its grand promises. Users quickly lost interest, and Ello faded into obscurity, becoming another footnote in the annals of social media failures.

Let's not forget the era of "Uber for X" and "Airbnb for Y". Startups were popping up left and right, promising to 'disrupt' every industry imaginable. Need an oil change for your car? There's an app for that. Want someone to walk your goldfish? There's probably an app for that too. The problem was, many of these startups failed to realize that not every industry needed disrupting, and not every service was improved by shoehorning it into an app.

It was as if Silicon Valley was stuck in a loop, and every entrepreneur was trying to recreate the magic of Uber or Airbnb for the most random and often ridiculous things.

Take "Washio", for example, the so-called "Uber for Laundry". The idea was simple: you order a laundry pickup and delivery through an app. Convenient? Absolutely. Sustainable business model? Not so much. After raising $16 million in funding, the company folded, proving that not every chore needs an app solution.

Or consider "HomeJoy", the "Uber for Cleaning". While the concept had potential, it was the execution where things went awry. They faced class-action lawsuits over worker classification, a common challenge for these gig economy models. Not to mention the operational headache of managing quality across a fleet of independent contractors. The company shuttered its operations after a few years, leaving behind a trail of unhappy customers and even unhappier cleaners.

And let's not forget the slew of "Airbnb for" startups that popped up. "Airbnb for dogs", "Airbnb for boats", "Airbnb for office space". It was as if they were tossing darts at a board of random nouns to find their business model.

In the end, these startups served as a reminder that copying a successful model and slapping it onto a different service isn't enough. It's not just about the technology; it's about understanding the market, the problem you're solving, and the nuances of the industry you're in. And as any grumpy entrepreneur will tell you, there's no shortcut for hard work, solid research, and a sprinkle of originality.

And who could forget the blockchain craze? Suddenly, everyone was trying to incorporate blockchain into their business, whether it made sense or not. It was like watching a toddler try to fit a square peg into a round hole - amusing, but ultimately futile.

Each of these trends brought its own set of challenges. From unsustainable business models and market oversaturation to regulatory hurdles and public skepticism, startups have had to navigate a minefield of obstacles. But hey, what doesn't kill you makes you stronger, right? Or in the case of startups, what doesn't bankrupt you makes you pivot.

Looking back, it's easy to laugh at some of these trends and the challenges they brought. But remember, hindsight is 20/20. At the time, each of these trends represented the 'next big thing,' the future of startups. So, while we chuckle at the ghosts of startups past, let's not forget the lessons they've taught us. Because as we all know, those who fail to learn from history are doomed to repeat it. And in the startup world, repeating history often means burning through a whole lot of cash. Now, on to the next chapter, and remember - no eye rolling, please.

2 The 2023 Startup Landscape: Challenges and Opportunities

2.1. Economic Factors and Market Volatility

LISTEN UP, BECAUSE we're getting serious here. No jokes, no wisecracks, just the cold, hard truth. You see, the world of startups isn't all ping-pong tables and beer fridges. It's an economic battlefield, and if you want to survive, you'd better understand the lay of the land.

The year is 2023, and things are, to put it mildly, interesting. We've got inflation behaving like a teenager at a rave, and interest rates doing a balancing act on a tightrope. The economy's recovering from a pandemic, and the market is about as stable as a house of cards in a wind tunnel.

Startups, like any other business, aren't immune to these economic factors. In fact, they might be more vulnerable. They don't have the reserves of the big players, or the diversified portfolios that can cushion the blow. For startups, an economic hiccup can feel like a full-on gut punch.

Market volatility, my friends, is the silent predator of the startup world. One minute, you're riding high on a wave of consumer demand and investor interest. The next, you're wiped out by an unexpected downturn or a shift in market sentiment. And let me tell you, there's nothing quite like watching your valuation drop faster than a lead balloon.

But, and it's a big 'but', market volatility isn't all doom and gloom. Oh no, it's also a breeding ground for opportunities. In an unstable market, the status quo gets a good shakeup. Consumer needs change, gaps appear in the market, and new niches emerge. For the agile startup, market volatility can be a golden ticket to innovation and growth.

Economic factors, too, can be a double-edged sword. Take inflation, for example. On the one hand, it increases your costs, squeezing your already tight margins. On the other hand, it might also increase the demand for innovative, cost-effective solutions - the bread and butter of the startup world.

So, there you have it. Economic factors and market volatility - the boogeymen of the startup world. They're scary, unpredictable, and utterly unavoidable. But remember, in the world of startups, every challenge is an opportunity in disguise. You just have to be brave enough, and smart enough, to seize it. Now, go forth and conquer, and for heaven's sake, keep an eye on those interest rates.

2.2. The Impact of COVID-19 and the Post-Pandemic World

OKAY, IT'S TIME TO talk about the elephant in the room - COVID-19. You know, that pesky little virus that turned the world upside down and shook the startup landscape like a snow globe. Let's delve into how it's changed the game for startups, and what the post-pandemic world has in store for us.

The pandemic was, to put it bluntly, a slap in the face for many startups. It tore up business plans, evaporated funding, and sent consumer demand into a tailspin. But, much like a grumpy entrepreneur faced with yet another pitch for a 'revolutionary' social media app, startups are nothing if not resilient.

Many startups took the pandemic as a challenge, a gauntlet thrown down by an uncaring universe. They pivoted, they innovated, they found ways to not only survive but thrive in the chaos. And those who managed to rise above the turmoil have started to reap the rewards in the post-pandemic world.

The impact of COVID-19 has brought about a seismic shift in what it means to be a 'successful' startup. It's no longer just about high valuations and rapid growth. Nowadays, resilience, adaptability, and social impact are the new buzzwords. And the startup awards, those shiny baubles coveted by founders and investors alike, are reflecting this shift.

Startups that demonstrated agility and resilience, that were able to pivot their business models to adapt to the new normal, are the ones grabbing the spotlight. They're the ones bagging awards for 'Best COVID Pivot' or 'Most Resilient Startup'.

Then there are the startups that stepped up and made a positive impact during the crisis. The ones who used their tech to help track the virus, support remote learning, or keep businesses running with digital solutions. They're being recognized with awards for 'Social Impact' and 'Innovation in Crisis Response'.

The post-pandemic world has also seen a rise in awards for startups focusing on mental health and remote work solutions - two areas that have become increasingly important in the wake of the pandemic.

So, yes, the impact of COVID-19 on the startup world was brutal. But it also forced us to rethink what we value in startups. It's not just about the bottom line anymore. It's about resilience, adaptability, and making a positive impact. And those are lessons worth carrying into the post-pandemic world.

As for the awards? Well, they're just the icing on the cake. But remember, even the shiniest award isn't worth a penny if you can't keep your startup afloat in the stormy seas of the real world. Now, let's move on, before I get too philosophical.

2.3. Technology Trends: AI, Machine Learning, and Automation

ALRIGHT, BUCKLE UP, because we're diving into the swirling vortex of buzzwords known as technology trends. I'm talking about AI, machine learning, and automation. You can't swing a cat in the startup world without hitting one of these terms. Not that I recommend swinging cats. That's a quick way to land yourself in hot water with the animal rights folks.

First off, AI, or artificial intelligence. A term that's thrown around so much, you'd think we're living in a science fiction novel. But let's get one thing straight - just because you've programmed your toaster to burn your initials into your bread doesn't mean you've created AI. True AI is about creating machines capable of performing tasks that normally require human intelligence. And no, deciding between rye or whole wheat doesn't count as a task requiring human intelligence.

Next up, machine learning. This is where your toaster starts learning from its mistakes and stops burning your toast. It's a type of AI that allows machines to learn from data, improving their performance without being explicitly programmed. It's like teaching a dog new tricks, only the dog is a computer and the tricks involve complex algorithms. Also, there's no treat at the end. Just more data.

Then we have automation. Now, I'm not talking about the kind of automation where you set your coffee maker to start brewing at 6 a.m. I'm talking about using technology to automate complex business processes. It's like having a virtual army of robotic minions handling the grunt work, freeing up the humans to do what they do best - complain about the coffee.

Now, these trends aren't just fancy buzzwords. They're game-changers, disruptors, the big kahunas of the tech world. They're transforming industries, redefining business models, and making life hell for anyone who can't keep up.

Startups are riding these trends like surfers on a monster wave. They're using AI to create personalized customer experiences, machine learning to crunch vast amounts of data, and automation to streamline operations. It's a brave new world, full of potential... and a whole lot of jargon.

But remember, with great power comes great responsibility. And by responsibility, I mean the potential for things to go hilariously wrong. Like when your AI-powered customer service chatbot starts recommending existentialist philosophy instead of your latest product. Or when your automated email system decides to spam your entire client list with pictures of your office dog. Ah, technology. It's a wonderful thing, until it isn't.

So there you have it, a grumpy entrepreneur's take on AI, machine learning, and automation. They're exciting, they're transformative, and they're as complex as a Rubik's cube. Now, if you'll excuse me, I need to go reset my toaster. It's started making toast at random intervals, and I'm starting to think it's trying to communicate.

2.4. Regulatory Hurdles and Legal Challenges

AH, REGULATIONS AND legal challenges, the thorns in every startup's side. They're like that overly cautious parent who insists on bubble-wrapping everything in sight. You appreciate their concern, but boy, do they know how to take the fun out of things.

Startups, especially those in the tech sector, often find themselves operating in uncharted territory. It's like exploring a new continent, only instead of wild animals and unpredictable weather, you're dealing with outdated laws and clueless regulators. One minute you're sailing along, the next you've run aground on a reef of red tape.

Take the sharing economy startups, for instance. They thought they'd hit upon the perfect business model, only to find themselves embroiled in legal battles over worker rights and zoning laws. It's like throwing a great party, only to have the cops show up because you didn't get a permit for your bonfire.

And let's not even get started on data privacy regulations. In the age of big data, startups are like kids in a candy store. So much delicious data to munch on! But then along comes GDPR, wagging its finger and slapping fines left and right. Suddenly, that candy starts to leave a bitter taste in your mouth.

Then there's the fun of intellectual property rights. You've spent months developing a revolutionary new product, only to find that some guy in a garage patented a similar idea ten years ago. Now you're facing a lawsuit and the only thing revolutionary is the amount of money you're going to owe in legal fees.

But it's not all doom and gloom. Navigating regulatory hurdles and legal challenges is part of the startup game. It's like an obstacle course, designed to separate the weak from the strong. The successful startups are the ones who can jump through the hoops without losing their balance.

So, my fellow entrepreneurs, don't let regulations and legal challenges get you down. Instead, see them as opportunities to show your mettle. Just remember to hire a good lawyer. And maybe keep a roll of bubble wrap handy, just in case. Now, onto the next challenge. After all, it wouldn't be a startup journey without a few bumps in the road.

2.5. Fundraising in an Uncertain Economy for 2023

WELL, WELL, WELL, IF it isn't the most nerve-wracking, hair-pulling, sleep-destroying aspect of running a startup: fundraising. Yes, gathering up the financial fuel to power your big dreams, especially in this roller coaster of an economy we're calling 2023. It's about as easy as nailing jelly to a wall.

In the good old days, you could slap together a flashy presentation, spout some buzzwords like 'disruption' and 'synergy', and investors would line up to throw money at you. These days, you'd be lucky if they throw you a sympathetic glance. The days of raising money from a powerpoint have gone.

You see, we're living in uncertain times. The economy's doing the cha-cha-cha on a tightrope, and investors are understandably skittish. They're clutching their wallets like life preservers on a sinking ship, and it's your job to convince them to toss them overboard.

Now, don't get me wrong. There's still plenty of money out there. It's just that investors have become pickier than a food critic at a fast food joint. They're looking for more than just a fancy pitch and a charismatic founder. They want to see traction, a robust business model, and a team that can execute. And even then, they might just offer you a term sheet that makes a loan shark seem like a philanthropist.

And let's not forget about the competition. With so many startups vying for the same pot of gold, the fundraising landscape has become a gladiator arena. Only instead of swords and shields, you're armed with pitch decks and term sheets. And trust me, the wounds from a rejected pitch can sting just as much as a gladiator's sword. Remember that most investors give a deck an initial 60seconds.

So how do you navigate this treacherous terrain? Well, first off, you've got to have a solid plan. A wish and a prayer just won't cut it. You need to show potential investors that you've got a clear path to profitability, even in this wacky economy. You need to show awareness of the current climate and not head in the sand.

Second, you've got to be resilient. You're going to hear 'no' a lot. Like, a LOT. But each 'no' gets you one step closer to a 'yes'. So, pick yourself up, dust off your ego, and keep going.

Thirdly , get use to preferences and ratchets. Ah, preferences and ratchets, the bread and butter of investment deals. Or should I say, the red flags and tripwires? These are the fine prints that can turn your sweet deal into a sour mess faster than you can say "valuation cap".

Let's start with preferences, or as I like to call them, the investor's safety net. These are typically in the form of liquidation preferences, which essentially means if things go belly up, the investor gets their money back before you see a dime. It's like going to a potluck dinner, but the investor gets to eat first, and you're left with whatever crumbs are left. Fair? Debatable. Common? Absolutely.

And then there are ratchets. No, not the tool, although they can be just as tightening. A ratchet is a clause that protects the investor if the company raises money at a lower valuation in the future. It's like a magic trick where the investor's share of the company increases without them having to invest another penny. Great for them, not so great for you.

Now, don't get me wrong, I'm not saying these are inherently evil. They're part of the risk and reward equation of the startup world. But as an entrepreneur, you need to be aware of them. You need to understand what you're signing up for, and how it might affect your future fundraising, your control over the company, and your potential payout.

So, the next time you're about to sign on that dotted line, take a moment to scrutinize those terms. Get a good lawyer, do your homework, and make sure you're not trading your unicorn dreams for a one-way ticket to Downroundville. Because in this high stakes game of startups, the devil is often in the details.

And finally, don't forget to keep a sense of humor. After all, if you can't laugh at the absurdity of pitching your heart out to a room full of poker-faced investors, you're in the wrong game.

Fundraising in an uncertain economy is tough, no doubt about it. But as the old saying goes, when the going gets tough, the tough get going. Or in the case of startups, the tough get fundraising. Now, go out there and show 'em what you're made of. And remember, no matter how many 'nos' you get, it only takes one 'yes' to change everything.

2.6. Case Studies of Startup Success and Failure in 2023

ALRIGHT FOLKS, GATHER 'round the campfire. It's story time. We're going to delve into some riveting tales of startup triumph and tragedy from the wild west of 2023. Grab your popcorn, because these stories have more twists and turns than a mountain road.

First up, let's talk about SuccessCo (yes, that's a placeholder name. Their actual name was some unpronounceable mashup of vowels and consonants, but for the sake of my sanity, we'll call them SuccessCo). They were the golden child of the startup scene, the ones who could do no wrong. They had a killer product, a star-studded team, and a business model that was tighter than a hipster's jeans. And, unlike many startups, they managed to turn a profit within their first year. Yes, you heard that right. A profit! In their first year! It was like spotting a unicorn in the wild.

Their secret? Well, they had a clear vision, a laser focus on their customers, and they didn't waste time chasing every shiny new trend that came along. They also had a knack for raising funds, even in the uncertain economy of 2023. They could charm the wallets out of investors' pockets faster than a street magician.

Now, let's turn our attention to the other side of the coin - FailTech (again, not their real name. Their actual name was something equally uninspiring, but let's not add insult to injury). They started with a bang, raising a hefty seed round and generating a lot of buzz in the tech press. They had a flashy office, a foosball table, and a CEO who could sell ice to Eskimos.

But, as we all know, buzz doesn't pay the bills. Their product, though innovative, was riddled with bugs. Their business model was about as stable as a Jenga tower, and their customer service was, well, let's just say it left a lot to be desired.

In the end, FailTech became a cautionary tale, a ghost story to tell newbie entrepreneurs around the campfire. Their downfall was a potent cocktail of overhype, underdelivery, and a lack of focus. They burned through their funds faster than a pyromaniac at a bonfire, and in the end, all they had to show for it was a fancy office and a very well-used foosball table.

So, what can we learn from these tales of success and failure? Well, it's simple really. In the startup world, hype can only take you so far. At the end of the day, you need a solid product, a sustainable business model, and a relentless focus on your customers. And a little bit of luck doesn't hurt either. Now, let's wrap up these stories and move on. After all, there's always another tale to tell in the startup world.

3 The 2024 Startup Landscape: Challenges and Opportunities

3.1. Predicted Economic and Market Trends in 2024 for Startups

OH, PREDICTING THE future. That's always a fun game. It's like trying to hit a bullseye on a moving target while blindfolded. But hey, as a grumpy entrepreneur, I'm always up for a challenge. So, let's take a wild swing at predicting the economic and market trends for startups in 2024.

First off, let's talk about the economy. Unless you've been living under a rock (which, considering the state of things, might not be such a bad idea), you know that we're in a pretty unpredictable economic climate. But here's the thing about economies - they're like pendulums. They swing back and forth, and right now, we're due for an upswing.

So, I predict that in 2024, we'll see a slow but steady economic recovery. It'll be like watching a snail race - frustratingly slow, but hey, at least it's moving in the right direction. This means that startups will have to continue being nimble, making do with less, and finding creative ways to stay afloat.

As for market trends, well, that's where things get interesting. Technology will continue to be the driving force behind most startups. I'm talking AI, machine learning, automation - all the usual suspects. But I also see a surge in interest around sustainability and social impact. Businesses that can marry tech innovation with environmental and social consciousness will be the belles of the ball.

Remote work is another trend that's here to stay. Thanks to our friend COVID-19, businesses have realized that they don't need fancy offices to be productive. This means more opportunities for startups to tap into global talent pools and less money spent on office space. It's a win-win situation, as long as you don't mind the occasional Zoom mishap.

Finally, I predict that customer-centric startups will shine in 2024. With so much competition out there, the businesses that truly understand and cater to their customers' needs will rise to the top. So, if you're not already obsessed with your customers, now's the time to start.

Well, there you have it, my predictions for 2024. Of course, take these with a grain of salt. The future is about as predictable as a cat on catnip. But as any seasoned entrepreneur will tell you, the key to navigating the future is flexibility, resilience, and a healthy dose of stubborn optimism. So, strap in, folks. 2024, here we come.

3.2. Emerging Technologies: Blockchain, Quantum Computing, and Beyond

AH, EMERGING TECHNOLOGIES. The shiny new toys of the business world. Every year, there's a new batch of buzzwords that make investors' hearts flutter and entrepreneurs' palms sweaty. This year, the buzz is all about blockchain and quantum computing. And let me tell you, it's about as easy to understand as a mime at a call center.

Let's start with blockchain. It's been around for a while, mostly as the backbone of cryptocurrencies like Bitcoin. But now, it's stepping into the spotlight as a technology that can revolutionize everything from supply chain management to voting systems. It's like that nerdy kid from high school who suddenly becomes the star quarterback.

So, what is blockchain? Well, imagine a ledger that's shared among a network of computers. Each transaction is recorded and verified by the network, making it nearly impossible to tamper with. It's like having a notary public on steroids.

Sounds great, right? But here's the catch. Implementing blockchain is about as straightforward as assembling IKEA furniture with chopsticks. It requires a hefty investment in time and resources, not to mention a deep understanding of the technology. So, before you jump on the blockchain bandwagon, make sure you know what you're getting into.

Next up, we have quantum computing. This is the big kahuna, the technology that could make our current computers look like abacuses. Quantum computers use the principles of quantum mechanics to process information, which basically means they can do complex calculations faster than you can say "quantum superposition". If I explain it a bit better .Consider this: a classical computer bit is a boring old stick in the mud - it's either a 1 or a 0, no in-betweens. But a quantum bit, a qubit, now that's a party animal. It can be a 1, a 0, or both at the same time! It's like Schrödinger's cat, but instead of being dead or alive, it's running Windows or Linux simultaneously. Mind-blowing, right?

Here's the kicker. It gets even wilder when you have multiple qubits. They can be entangled in such a way that the state of one qubit can depend on the state of another, no matter how far they are. It's like having twins who feel each other's pain, but on a subatomic level. Spooky!

Just imagine the possibilities! Need to factor a large number for encryption? No problem, a quantum computer could do it before you can say "quantum supremacy". Want to simulate molecular interactions for drug discovery? Easy peasy, just throw some qubits at it.

But here's the grumpy reality check. We're still a long way off from quantum computers becoming mainstream. Right now, they're more unstable than a startup's cash flow and require temperatures colder than deep space to work. So, unless you have a dilution fridge and a team of quantum physicists handy, I wouldn't start converting your data centers just yet.

But don't rush to upgrade your office computers just yet. Quantum computing is still in its infancy, and there are more kinks to iron out than in a second-hand slinky. Plus, there's the small matter of quantum computers being more expensive than a beachfront property in Monaco.

So, should your startup invest in these emerging technologies? Well, that's like asking if you should buy a racehorse. It could win you the Grand National, or it could eat all your carrots and poop in your shoes. The key is to thoroughly understand the technology and its potential impact on your business before taking the plunge.

Remember, the goal isn't to chase every shiny new toy. It's to find the right tools to solve your customers' problems. If blockchain or quantum computing can do that, then by all means, go for it. Just make sure you have a hefty stash of aspirin on hand for the inevitable headaches.

3.3. Evolving Regulatory Frameworks

AH, REGULATIONS. THE red tape that wraps itself around the entrepreneurial spirit like an overzealous python. But let's face it, without regulations, the business world would be more chaotic than a toddler's birthday party. So, let's dive into the thrilling, adrenaline-fueled world of evolving regulatory frameworks for 2024.

First, let's tackle the big, scary beast in the room - data privacy. Ever since the GDPR reared its head in Europe, data privacy has become the hot potato of the tech world. And it's not going away anytime soon. If anything, regulations around data privacy are set to become stricter. This means that startups will have to be more transparent about how they collect and use customer data, or face fines that could make a pirate's treasure look like pocket change.

Next up, we have regulations around cryptocurrencies and blockchain technology. Now, I'm no fortune teller, but I predict that 2024 will see tighter regulations in this space. Governments around the world are starting to realize that cryptocurrencies aren't just for buying pizza and illicit goods on the internet. They're becoming mainstream, and with that comes the need for regulation. So, if your startup is operating in this space, you'd better get cozy with the legal eagles.

Now, let's turn our attention to the gig economy. With remote work becoming the norm, more people are turning to freelance and contract work. This is leading to a shift in labor laws, with more emphasis on protecting the rights of gig workers. Startups will need to navigate this changing landscape, balancing the need for flexible labor with the need to provide fair working conditions.

And finally, let's not forget about environmental regulations. With climate change looming like a grumpy bear fresh out of hibernation, governments are cracking down on environmental offenders. This means stricter regulations around emissions, waste management, and energy use. Green startups, or those that can adapt to these changes, will be at a distinct advantage.

Navigating these evolving regulatory frameworks won't be easy. It's like playing a game of Twister, where the dots keep moving and the spinner is controlled by a caffeinated squirrel. But with a solid understanding of the rules, a flexible approach, and a good lawyer on speed dial, startups can turn these challenges into opportunities.

Remember, the goal isn't just to comply with regulations. It's to build a business that respects its customers, its employees, and the planet. Do that, and you'll not only survive the regulatory maze of 2024, you'll thrive in it.

3.5. Anticipated Challenges in Talent Acquisition and Retention in 2024

GATHER 'ROUND, ENTREPRENEURS, and let's talk about the mythical creatures known as "talent". These elusive beings are the lifeblood of your startup, but catching and keeping them is about as easy as herding cats. And with the way things are going, 2024 is shaping up to be quite the safari. So, strap in, and let's navigate the wild world of talent acquisition and retention.

First up, we have the challenge of finding the right talent. You see, in the startup world, we're not just looking for any old employee. No, we're hunting for unicorns, those magical beings who have the right mix of skills, attitude, and the ability to survive on a diet of instant ramen and energy drinks.

But here's the thing. These unicorns? They're in high demand. And they know it. They're more likely to be wooed by the Googles and Amazons of the world, with their fancy offices, high salaries, and perks that make your startup look like a lemonade stand.

So how do you lure these unicorns to your startup? Well, you've got to offer them something they can't get at a big corporation. Maybe it's the chance to make a real impact, or the opportunity to work on cutting-edge technology. Or maybe it's just free donuts on Fridays. Whatever it is, you need to find it and flaunt it.

Now, let's talk about retention. So, you've caught your unicorn. Congrats! But don't start celebrating just yet. Because keeping that unicorn is another challenge altogether.

In the fast-paced world of startups, burnout is as common as coffee stains on keyboard. Long hours, high stress, and the constant pressure to perform can send your unicorns galloping for the exit. To keep them around, you'll need to create a work environment that's not only challenging and exciting, but also supportive and flexible.

And let's not forget about career development. Your unicorns aren't just looking for a job. They're looking for a career. A journey. A saga worthy of a Netflix series. If they can't see a future at your startup, they'll start looking for greener pastures.

So, there you have it. The wild and wooly world of talent acquisition and retention in 2024. It's not for the faint of heart. But if you can navigate it successfully, you'll have a team of unicorns that will make your startup shine. And isn't that worth a few sleepless nights and a lifetime supply of donuts?

3.6. Predicted Case Studies: Potential Winners and Losers of 2024 Startup Scene

WELL, WELL, WELL. NOW we're getting into the juicy stuff. Predicting the winners and losers of the 2024 startup scene. It's a bit like trying to predict the weather in London. You can take a guess, but don't be surprised if it rains when you least expect it. But hey, I'm game if you are. So, let's shake our magic 8-ball and see what comes up.

First, the potential winners.

Winner Predict #1: Sustainable Tech Startups

With climate change being a grumpier beast than yours truly, sustainable tech startups are poised for success. Whether it's renewable energy, clean transportation, or eco-friendly manufacturing, startups that help save the planet while making a tidy profit are likely to be the toast of 2024. But remember, greenwashing won't cut it. It needs to be sustainable, not just sound sustainable.

Winner Predict #2: Health Tech Startups

If the COVID-19 pandemic taught us anything, it's that health tech is crucial. Startups that can leverage AI, machine learning, and big data to improve healthcare delivery and outcomes will be in a prime position. Think telemedicine, personalized medicine, mental health apps, and anything else that makes healthcare more accessible and efficient.

Winner Predict #3: Remote Work Solutions

With remote work becoming as common as coffee in the workplace, startups that offer innovative solutions to the challenges of remote work could hit the jackpot. This could include anything from project management tools to virtual reality conferencing systems. And don't forget about solutions that help maintain company culture and employee wellbeing.

Now, onto the potential losers.

Loser Predict #1: Gig Economy Startups

While the gig economy isn't going anywhere, the golden age of gig economy startups might be over. Increasing regulations and growing awareness of worker rights could mean tougher times for these businesses. Those that can't adapt to provide better conditions for their workers might find themselves out in the cold.

Loser Predict #2: Non-Secure Tech Startups

Startups that play fast and loose with data security are in for a rough ride. With stricter data protection regulations and growing consumer awareness about data privacy, a data breach could be a death sentence for these businesses.

Loser Predict #3: Over-Hyped AI Startups

AI is the buzzword du jour, but not all AI startups will make the cut. Those that promise the moon but deliver a slice of moldy cheese could find themselves facing investor wrath. The winners will be those that can demonstrate real value, not just flashy tech.

Remember, these are just predictions. The startup world is as unpredictable as a toddler on a sugar high. The key to success is adaptability, resilience, and a willingness to learn from both the victories and the failures. So, here's to the winners and losers of 2024. May the odds be ever in your favor.

4 The Future: Startup Challenges in 2025

4.1. Long-Term Economic and Market Predictions

AH, THE FUTURE. THAT mysterious, nebulous space where all our hopes, dreams, and fears reside. It's also the place where we hope to cash out our startup equity and retire to a life of luxury. But, alas, predicting the economic and market trends of 2025 is a bit like trying to predict the plot twists in a soap opera. However, as your ever-grumpy guide, I shall attempt to do just that.

First up, the economy. Now, I'm not an economist, but I do have a knack for spotting trends, and it seems the global economy is about as stable as a one-legged elephant on a tightrope. However, if current trends hold, we can expect a few key themes to dominate in 2025.

Theme #1: Sustainable Economy

With Mother Nature getting crankier by the year, there's a growing push for a sustainable economy. This means more emphasis on green technologies, renewable energy, and sustainable business practices. Startups that can't figure out how to make a profit without trashing the planet might find themselves out of favor with investors and customers alike.

Theme #2: Digital Economy

If you thought the digital revolution was over, think again. The digital economy is still in its toddler years, and we can expect more growth in 2025. This means more opportunities for startups in the digital space, but also more competition. So, sharpen your digital swords and prepare for battle.

Theme #3: Inclusive Economy

In 2025, the economy won't just be about making money. It'll be about making money in a way that's fair and inclusive. That means more focus on diversity, equal pay, and social impact. If your startup's idea of diversity is having different types of coffee in the break room, you might need to rethink your strategy.

Now, let's talk about market predictions. In 2025, the market will be more crowded, more competitive, and more global than ever before. Startups will need to be agile, innovative, and ready to pivot at a moment's notice. Remember, in the startup world, adaptability isn't just a nice-to-have, it's a must-have.

In summary, 2025 will be a wild ride. There will be challenges, there will be opportunities, and there will be more buzzwords than you can shake a stick at. But with a clear vision, a solid strategy, and a touch of stubborn optimism, your startup can not only survive the future but thrive in it. So buckle up, entrepreneurs. The future is coming, whether we're ready or not.

4.2. The Future of Technology: The Role of Innovation in Startup Success

WELL, WELL, WELL. THE future of technology. Now, there's a topic that's as expansive as the universe and just as mysterious. But fear not, dear entrepreneurs, your grumpy guide is here to steer you through this nebulous galaxy of innovation and gadgets.

First things first. The role of innovation in startup success. It's like the role of caffeine in startup culture. Absolutely, undeniably, and irrefutably crucial. If you're not innovating, you're stagnating. And there's nothing the market hates more than stagnation. It's like finding a fly in your soup, completely unappetizing.

So, what kind of technological marvels can we expect in 2025? Well, if I had a crystal ball, I'd be on a beach somewhere, sipping a margarita, not writing this book. But, based on current trends, here are a few educated guesses.

Guess #1: AI Everywhere

Artificial intelligence is already spreading like a spilled cup of coffee, seeping into every corner of our lives. By 2025, AI will be as common as overpriced coffee in a startup office. It'll be in our homes, our cars, our workplaces, even in our toilets (smart toilets, anyone?). But remember, it's not enough to slap AI on a product and call it innovative. It needs to add real value. And preferably not become our robot overlords.

Guess #2: Quantum Computing

Quantum computing is currently in the "I'm not quite sure what it is, but it sounds cool" stage. But by 2025, it could be a game-changer. Quantum computers could potentially solve problems that are beyond the reach of traditional computers. So, if your startup can ride the quantum wave, you could be in for a quantum leap in success.

Guess #3: Virtual and Augmented Reality

Virtual and augmented reality technologies are on the brink of becoming mainstream. By 2025, they could transform everything from gaming and entertainment to education and healthcare. Imagine a virtual reality meeting where you can interact with colleagues as if you're in the same room, or an augmented reality app that can show you how a piece of furniture will look in your home. If your startup can leverage these technologies, you could be on to a winner.

Guess #4 : Internet of Things (IoT)

With the advent of 5G and possibly 6G, IoT devices will become more interconnected, leading to smarter homes, cities, and industries. We can expect advancements in real-time data analysis and decision-making.

Guess #5 : Biotechnology

From gene editing technologies like CRISPR to advancements in personalized medicine and synthetic biology, biotech is a rapidly evolving field that could see significant breakthroughs by 2025.

Guess #6 : Sustainable Tech

Given the increasing global focus on climate change and sustainability, we can expect substantial evolution in clean energy technologies, carbon capture and storage, and other green technologies.

Guess #7 : Blockchain and Cryptocurrencies

Beyond Bitcoin and Ethereum, the underlying blockchain technology could find more mainstream applications, especially in areas like supply chain management, secure voting systems, digital identities, and more.

Guess #8 : Edge Computing

As the amount of data we produce continues to grow, edge computing - processing data closer to where it is generated (the "edge" of the network) rather than in a centralized location - may become increasingly important.

In conclusion, the future of technology is bright, shiny, and packed with potential. But remember, technology is just a tool. It's how you use it that counts. So, keep innovating, keep experimenting, and keep pushing the boundaries. After all, today's crazy idea could be tomorrow's game-changer. And with that, I'll see you in the future. Just don't forget to bring your hoverboard.

4.3. The Evolving Global Regulatory Landscape in 2025

NOW, I KNOW WHAT YOU'RE thinking. "Regulations, really? Isn't that as exciting as watching paint dry?" But bear with me, because if there's one thing that can throw a wrench in your startup dreams, it's running afoul of regulations. And in 2025, the regulatory landscape is going to be as complex and changeable as a Rubik's cube.

First up, let's talk about data privacy. Remember when you could just collect data willy-nilly without a care in the world? Yeah, those days are long gone. In 2025, data privacy regulations are going to be stricter than ever. And they're going to be global. So, if you're planning on collecting, using, or storing data, you'd better have a solid data privacy strategy in place. And I don't mean just ticking a box on a form. I mean actually understanding and complying with the regulations.

Next, let's talk about AI and automation. These technologies are advancing faster than a cheetah on roller skates, and regulators are scrambling to keep up. By 2025, we can expect new regulations governing the use of AI and automation, especially in areas like employment, privacy, and security. If your startup is in this space, you'll need to stay on top of these regulations or risk getting left in the dust.

Now, onto sustainability. With climate change becoming a critical issue, there's a growing push for sustainable business practices. In 2025, this could translate into new regulations requiring businesses to reduce their environmental impact. If your startup isn't green, you could find yourself in hot water.

And let's not forget about the gig economy. The rise of gig work has been a game-changer for many startups, but it's also raised some serious regulatory issues. By 2025, we can expect more regulations aimed at protecting gig workers, which could impact startups that rely on this model.

In summary, the regulatory landscape of 2025 is going to be a minefield of challenges and opportunities. Navigating it successfully will require a solid understanding of the regulations, a flexible approach, and a willingness to adapt. So, buckle up, entrepreneurs. It's going to be a bumpy ride. But with the right approach, you can turn regulatory challenges into competitive advantages. Now, isn't that a thrilling thought?

4.4. Future of Work: Remote Work, Gig

Economy, and New Employment Models

AH, THE FUTURE OF WORK. An elusive concept that's sparked more debates than a controversial referee call in a football match. Will we all be working from our homes, in our pajamas, with our pets as our only coworkers? Or will the gig economy turn us all into freelance warriors, battling for gigs in the vast wilderness of the internet? And what about new employment models? Are full-time contracts going the way of the dinosaur? Let's dive into this murky sea of uncertainty and try to fish out some answers.

Remote Work: The New Normal or a Passing Fad?

Remote work has become as popular as a viral cat video. But is it here to stay? In my grumpy opinion, yes. By 2025, the number of remote workers is likely to grow, not shrink. Why? Because it's convenient, it's cost-effective, and it allows you to work in your pajamas. What's not to love? Of course, it also means dealing with dodgy internet connections, Zoom fatigue, and the constant temptation of the fridge. But hey, no model is perfect.

Gig Economy: A Boon or a Bane?

The gig economy is like the wild west of the employment world. It offers freedom, flexibility, and the opportunity to be your own boss. But it also comes with uncertainty, instability, and the risk of being underpaid and overworked. By 2025, the gig economy is set to grow, but with greater regulation and a growing emphasis on worker rights. So, if you're a startup relying on gig workers, be prepared to offer fair pay, decent working conditions, and maybe even some benefits. Shocking, I know.

New Employment Models: Innovation or Exploitation?

New employment models are popping up like mushrooms after a rainstorm. We've got part-time, flextime, job sharing, zero-hours contracts, and more. These models offer flexibility and can be a good fit for certain roles and industries. But there's a fine line between innovation and exploitation. By 2025, startups will need to ensure their employment models are fair, transparent, and in line with regulatory requirements. Otherwise, they could find themselves on the wrong side of a lawsuit. And trust me, that's not a fun place to be.

In conclusion, the future of work is as certain as the British weather. But whatever happens, one thing is clear. The traditional 9-to-5, office-based work model is evolving. So, whether you're a fan of remote work, a gig economy enthusiast, or an advocate for new employment models, buckle up. The future of work is going to be a wild ride. Just remember to keep your employees' wellbeing at the heart of your decisions. After all, a happy employee is a productive employee. Even if they're working in their pajamas.

4.5. Sustainability and Climate Change: The Green Startup Revolution

GATHER AROUND, ENTREPRENEURS, it's time to talk about the elephant in the room. No, not the one about your dwindling coffee supply. I'm talking about sustainability and climate change. It's a topic that's hotter than a summer heatwave, and it's sparking a revolution in the startup world. So, put on your green hats and let's dive into the green startup revolution.

The first thing to understand is that sustainability isn't a fad, it's not a trend, and it's definitely not something you can ignore. It's as real as the mountains of plastic in our oceans and as urgent as the rising global temperatures. By 2025, ignoring sustainability will be as outdated as using a typewriter in your office.

So, what does this mean for startups? Well, it means that green is the new black. If your startup isn't thinking about sustainability, it's like trying to row a boat with a spoon. You're not going to get very far.

It's not just about reducing your carbon footprint, though that's important. It's about integrating sustainability into every aspect of your business. From the products or services you offer, to the way you operate, to the culture you foster. It's about understanding that profit and the planet are not mutually exclusive. In fact, they can, and should, go hand in hand.

But here's the thing about the green revolution. It's not just about doing the right thing. It's also about business survival. Consumers are becoming more environmentally conscious. They're demanding more from businesses and are willing to put their money where their mouth is. If your startup isn't meeting their green expectations, they're likely to take their business elsewhere.

And it's not just consumers. Investors are also hopping on the green bandwagon. They're looking to invest in startups that are sustainable, responsible, and profitable. So, if you're seeking funding, having a strong sustainability strategy can give you a competitive edge.

In conclusion, the green startup revolution is here, and it's changing the business landscape in ways we're only beginning to understand. By 2025, sustainability won't be an optional extra, it'll be a business imperative. So, get on board the green revolution, or get left behind. The choice is yours. Just remember, the future of our planet depends on the choices we make today. And that's a responsibility we all share. Even grumpy entrepreneurs like me.

4.6. Predicted Case Studies: Who Will Lead the Pack in 2025?

AH, PREDICTIONS. THE stuff of fortune tellers and horoscopes. But, as your trusty, if somewhat grumpy, guide, I'll do my best to gaze into my crystal ball and give you a glimpse into the future. So, without further ado, let's dive into the potential leaders of the pack in 2025.

The Sustainability Superstars

These are the startups that have embraced the green revolution with both hands. They're not just reducing their carbon footprint, they're actively working towards a positive environmental impact. They understand that sustainability isn't a buzzword, it's a business strategy. And it's paying off. Consumers love them, investors love them, and even Mother Nature is giving them a thumbs up.

The AI Innovators

Artificial Intelligence. The two words that have been on everyone's lips for the past decade. But by 2025, it's the startups that have moved beyond the hype and truly harnessed the power of AI that will be leading the pack. They're using AI to solve real problems, create real value, and drive real growth. And they're doing it in a way that's ethical, transparent, and socially responsible. Now, that's what I call smart.

The Remote Work Warriors

These startups have taken remote work and run with it. They've built a culture that's flexible, inclusive, and productive, regardless of where their employees are based. They've embraced technology, fostered communication, and prioritized well-being. As a result, they've attracted top talent, boosted employee engagement, and improved their bottom line. Who needs an office, anyway?

The Gig Economy Game-Changers

In the world of gig work, these startups are making waves. They've found a way to provide gig workers with the flexibility they crave, while also offering the stability and benefits usually reserved for full-time employees. It's a win-win situation, and it's shaking up the gig economy as we know it.

The Regulatory Mavericks

These startups are navigating the complex world of regulations with the finesse of a ballet dancer. They're not just complying with regulations, they're staying one step ahead. They're anticipating changes, adapting quickly, and turning potential regulatory hurdles into strategic opportunities. In the wild west of the startup world, these are the sheriffs.

So, there you have it. A sneak peek into the potential leaders of the pack in 2025. Of course, this is all speculation. The future is as unpredictable as a game of roulette. But one thing's for sure. The startups that adapt, innovate, and stay true to their values will be the ones that come out on top. And who knows, maybe your startup will be one of them. Now, wouldn't that be something?

5. Strategies for Future-Proofing Your Startup

5.1. Adopting Agile Business Models: Future-Proofing Your Startup

AH, THE AGILE BUSINESS model. A term that's been thrown around so much, it's starting to sound like a pop song chorus. But strip away the buzzwords and hype, and you've got a concept that's as solid as a pair of well-worn boots. But how can it help future-proof your startup? And how do you adopt it without turning your business into a game of Twister? Strap in, entrepreneurs, we're about to find out.

Understanding Agility: It's Not Just for Gymnasts

Let's start with the basics. What does it mean to be agile? No, it doesn't mean being able to do a backflip (though that's impressive). In the business world, agility means being able to adapt quickly and effectively to changes. It means having a business model that's as flexible as a yoga instructor.

The Agile Advantage: Dodging Metaphorical Bullets

An agile business model can give your startup a competitive edge. It allows you to respond quickly to changes in the market, customer needs, or even the regulatory landscape. It's like having a bullet-dodging superpower. A new competitor pops up? Dodge. A sudden market shift? Dodge. A change in regulations? Dodge. You get the idea.

Implementing Agility: A Balancing Act

But how do you implement an agile business model? Well, it's a bit like balancing on a tightrope. On one side, you've got structure and consistency. On the other, flexibility and adaptability. Lean too far one way, and you'll fall into chaos. Lean too far the other, and you'll become rigid and inflexible.

Finding the balance requires a few key ingredients. First, you need a clear vision and strategy. This acts as your north star, guiding your decisions and actions. Second, you need a flexible organizational structure. This allows you to adapt and change without getting tied up in red tape. Third, you need a culture that embraces change and fosters innovation. This encourages your team to think outside the box and come up with creative solutions.

Agility in Action: A Startup Survival Kit

So, what does an agile business model look like in practice? It could mean adopting a lean startup approach, where you launch quickly, gather feedback, and iterate. It could mean embracing remote work or flexible working arrangements. It could mean diversifying your product or service offerings. Or it could mean partnering with other businesses to tap into new markets or technologies.

In conclusion, adopting an agile business model is like packing a survival kit for your startup. It equips you with the tools you need to navigate the unpredictable terrain of the business world. It won't make the journey easy, but it'll make it possible. And in the world of startups, that's half the battle. So, get out there and start flexing your agility muscles. The future is waiting.

5.2. Leveraging Emerging Technologies: Or, How to Not Get Left in the Digital Dust

Ah, technology. It's changing faster than a chameleon on a rainbow, and if you're not careful, you might just get left in the digital dust. As an entrepreneur, it's your job to stay ahead of the curve, to leverage these emerging technologies, to ride the wave of digital innovation without wiping out. Sounds fun, right? Let's dive in.

Cutting Through the Tech Talk

First things first. You need to cut through the tech talk. Blockchain, AI, IoT, VR, AR, MR – it's like alphabet soup up here. But don't get lost in the acronyms. Your job isn't to become a tech whiz, it's to understand how these technologies can benefit your startup.

Technological Tools, Not Toys

Just because a technology is shiny and new doesn't mean it's right for your startup. Remember, these are tools, not toys. So before you jump on the latest tech trend, ask yourself: How will this technology help my startup? Will it improve efficiency? Enhance customer experience? Open up new markets? If you can't answer these questions, it might be best to steer clear.

One Small Step for Tech, One Giant Leap for Your Startup

When it comes to leveraging emerging technologies, you don't have to take a giant leap. Start small. Experiment. Test. Learn. Remember, Rome wasn't built in a day, and neither is a tech-savvy startup. So, whether it's integrating AI into your customer service or using blockchain for data security, take one step at a time.

Don't Go It Alone

Navigating the world of emerging technologies can feel like trekking through a jungle. So, don't go it alone. Find a guide. This could be a tech consultant, a savvy new hire, or even a tech-forward partner company. With the right guide, you can avoid the pitfalls and find the path to success.

Stay Ahead, But Stay Grounded

While it's important to stay ahead of the tech curve, it's just as important to stay grounded. Don't lose sight of your vision, your mission, or your customers. Technology is there to support your startup, not to drive it. Keep your feet on the ground and your head in the clouds (preferably a secure, efficient cloud platform).

In conclusion, leveraging emerging technologies is like surfing. It's about balance, timing, and a healthy dose of bravery. And remember, even if you wipe out, you can always get back on the board. So, paddle out, catch a wave, and ride the tech tide to startup success. Just remember to wear your digital sunscreen.

5.3. Building a Resilient and Diverse Team: Or, How to Create a Startup Dream Team Without Losing Your Mind

AH, TEAM BUILDING. The two words that can send a shiver down any entrepreneur's spine. You see, building a team isn't like assembling IKEA furniture. There's no instruction manual, no neatly labeled parts, and certainly no Allen wrench. But don't despair, dear entrepreneurs. Building a resilient and diverse team is possible, and I'm here to guide you through it. So, grab a cup of coffee (or something stronger), and let's get started.

Resilience: More Than Just a Buzzword

First things first. What does it mean to have a resilient team? No, it doesn't mean they bounce when you drop them (please, don't try that). Resilience is about coping with change, facing challenges, and bouncing back from setbacks. It's about adaptability, flexibility, and tenacity. And in the fast-paced world of startups, it's a must-have.

So, how do you build a resilient team? Well, it starts with hiring. Look for people who are problem solvers, who aren't afraid of failure, and who have a track record of bouncing back. But it doesn't stop there. You need to foster resilience, through a supportive culture, open communication, and opportunities for growth and learning.

Diversity: The Secret Sauce of Startup Success

Next up, diversity. Now, I'm not just talking about ticking boxes or filling quotas. Diversity isn't just a nice-to-have, it's a need-to-have. A diverse team brings different perspectives, ideas, and experiences to the table. It fuels creativity, innovation, and problem-solving. In short, it's the secret sauce of startup success.

Building a diverse team isn't just about hiring diverse individuals. It's about creating an inclusive culture where everyone feels valued, heard, and respected. It's about breaking down barriers, challenging biases, and embracing differences. And it's about walking the walk, not just talking the talk.

The Dynamic Duo: Resilience and Diversity

When you combine resilience and diversity, you get a team that's not just strong, but adaptable. A team that can handle whatever the startup world throws at them. A team that can innovate, pivot, and persevere. It's like having your own startup Avengers.

Building a resilient and diverse team is no small feat. It takes time, effort, and a hefty dose of patience. But trust me, it's worth it. Because at the end of the day, a startup is only as strong as its team. So, invest in your team, nurture them, and watch as they take your startup to new heights. And remember, even in the grumpiest of times, a strong team can be the beacon of hope that guides you to success.

5.4. Fundraising in the Future: Alternatives to Traditional Venture Capital, or "Show Me the Money... Differently!"

OH, FUNDRAISING. THE thrilling roller coaster ride that every startup founder loves to hate. It's like a game show where the stakes are your company, your sanity, and your ability to look at another spreadsheet without bursting into tears. But fear not, brave entrepreneurs, the future of fundraising is here, and it's not just about cozying up to VCs anymore. So buckle up, and let's dive into the exciting world of alternative fundraising.

Crowdfunding: Because Two Pockets are Better Than One

First up, we have crowdfunding. It's like throwing a party where everyone brings you money instead of cheap wine and stale chips. Websites like Kickstarter and Indiegogo have made it possible for the

Average Joes of the world to back your idea. But remember, with great power comes great responsibility - and a horde of internet strangers asking for updates and wondering why their perk hasn't arrived yet.

ICO: When Blockchain Met Fundraising

Then there's the Initial Coin Offering, or ICO. It's like an IPO, but instead of shares, investors get tokens, and instead of a regulated market, you get the Wild West of blockchain. It's high risk, high reward, and high chances of getting lost in a sea of crypto-jargon. But for those brave enough to venture into the blockchain frontier, it can be a lucrative path.

Revenue-Based Financing: Show Me the Money...Later

Revenue-based financing is like your rich uncle lending you money, but instead of awkward family dinners, you pay him back with a portion of your revenues. It's a great option if you're generating cash but aren't keen on giving away equity. Just make sure you've got a solid plan to increase those revenues, or you might find yourself in a cash crunch.

Bootstrapping: DIY Fundraising

And let's not forget about bootstrapping. It's the DIY approach to fundraising, where you fund your startup with your savings, your revenue, or your grandma's secret cookie recipe. It's not easy, and it might involve living on ramen noodles for a while, but it gives you control and keeps you out of the VC shark tank.

The Future is Now: Choose Your Own Fundraising Adventure

So there you have it, folks. The future of fundraising is here, and it's as diverse as a bag of jelly beans. As an entrepreneur, it's your job to choose the method that's right for you and your startup. And remember, whether you're crowdfunding, ICO-ing, revenue-financing, or bootstrapping, it's all about the hustle. So, get out there and show them the money!

5.5. Navigating Regulatory Changes: Or, How to Dodge Legal Landmines Without Losing Your Cool

AH, REGULATIONS. NOTHING gets an entrepreneur's heart pounding quite like the thought of wading through reams of legal jargon and regulatory frameworks. It's like trying to solve a Rubik's Cube in the dark while juggling flaming torches. But fear not, intrepid startup owners, for navigating regulatory changes is a skill that can be mastered, and I'm here to show you how.

Stay Informed: Knowledge is Power

The first rule of navigating regulatory changes is to stay informed. Laws and regulations can change as often as your teenager's mood, so it's essential to keep your finger on the pulse. This could mean subscribing to industry newsletters, joining relevant online communities, or even hiring a legal consultant. The key is to stay ahead of the game so that you're not blindsided by changes.

Understand the Impact: Your Startup Under the Legal Microscope

Not all regulatory changes will affect your startup in the same way. It's important to understand the potential impact of each change on your business operations, finances, and strategic direction. This might involve some detective work, a bit of crystal ball gazing, and a whole lot of coffee. But remember, forewarned is forearmed.

Be Agile: Regulatory Limbo is Not a Dance

When regulatory changes come knocking, it's essential to be agile. This doesn't mean touching your toes (though a bit of yoga never hurt anyone), but rather being able to adapt quickly and efficiently. This might involve tweaking your business model, updating your policies, or even pivoting your strategy. Being agile is about staying on your toes, even when the regulatory ground is shifting beneath you.

Build a Compliance Culture: Everyone's on the Legal Team

Finally, navigating regulatory changes isn't just the job of your legal department. Everyone in your startup should be aware of the importance of compliance and be ready to adapt to changes. This means fostering a compliance culture, offering training and support, and encouraging open communication. After all, compliance is a team sport.

In conclusion, navigating regulatory changes can be a daunting task. But with the right approach, it doesn't have to be a startup nightmare. Stay informed, understand the impact, be agile, and build a compliance culture, and you'll be dodging those legal landmines like a pro. And remember, in the world of startups, the only constant is change. So, embrace it, navigate it, and let it drive your startup to new heights.

5.6. The Importance of Sustainability and Corporate Social Responsibility: Or, How to Save the World and Your Startup at the Same Time

AH, SUSTAINABILITY and corporate social responsibility (CSR), the two buzzwords that have taken the business world by storm. They're like the kale and quinoa of the startup world - not always the most appetizing, but darn good for you. But fear not, intrepid entrepreneurs, because embracing sustainability and CSR doesn't have to be a bitter pill to swallow. In fact, it can be a delicious recipe for startup success. So, grab your superhero cape, and let's save the world.

Sustainability: More Than Just Hugging Trees

First up, let's talk about sustainability. Now, I'm not just talking about recycling your coffee cups or turning off the lights (though you should definitely do those things). Sustainability is about ensuring your startup has a positive impact on the environment, the community, and the economy. It's about thinking long-term, beyond your quarterly profits. And it's about recognizing that your startup is part of a bigger ecosystem, and what's good for the ecosystem is good for you.

CSR: Doing Good is Good Business

Next, let's tackle CSR. It's like being the good guy in a superhero movie - you help people, you improve the community, and you get to wear a cool logo. But CSR isn't just about philanthropy. It's about how your startup interacts with its stakeholders - from your employees to your customers to your suppliers. It's about ethics, fairness, and transparency. And in a world where reputation is everything, CSR can be your secret weapon.

The Dynamic Duo: Sustainability and CSR

When you combine sustainability and CSR, you get a startup that's not just profitable, but also beneficial. You attract loyal customers who love what you stand for. You attract talented employees who want to work for a company that makes a difference. And you attract investors who understand that sustainable and responsible businesses are a smart bet.

So, how do you embrace sustainability and CSR? It starts with your values. Make them a part of your mission, your strategy, and your daily operations. Communicate them to your stakeholders, and hold yourself accountable. And remember, sustainability and CSR aren't just checkboxes to tick or PR stunts to pull. They're commitments to making the world a better place, one startup at a time.

In conclusion, sustainability and CSR aren't just important - they're essential. They're the keys to a successful, responsible, and respected startup. So, embrace them, invest in them, and let them guide your startup to a future that's not just profitable, but also bright, green, and fair. And remember, as an entrepreneur, you're not just building a business. You're building a legacy. So, make it a good one.

6. Conclusion

6.1. The Resilience of the Startup Ecosystem: Or, How Startups are Like Cockroaches (But in a Good Way!)

AH, THE STARTUP ECOSYSTEM. It's a wild, chaotic, unpredictable jungle out there. One moment you're the king of the world, the next you're fighting off a pack of venture capitalists with nothing but your pitch deck and an ergonomic keyboard. But through it all, the startup ecosystem remains resilient. It's like a cockroach in the face of a nuclear explosion, and I mean that in the nicest possible way.

The Startup Species: Survival of the Fittest

Firstly, let's talk about startups themselves. They're the ultimate survivors. They're born in basements and coffee shops, raised on ramen noodles and caffeine, and evolve faster than a strain of the common cold. They're the cockroaches of the business world - adaptable, tenacious, and remarkably hard to squash.

The Entrepreneurial Instinct: Adapting to Anything

And what about entrepreneurs? They're the captains of this resilient ship. They navigate storms of market volatility, dodge icebergs of regulatory change, and patch up leaks in their business models with duct tape and a can-do attitude. They can pivot faster than a ballet dancer and adapt quicker than a chameleon in a paint factory. They're the heart and soul of the startup ecosystem's resilience.

The Supportive Ecosystem: A Jungle Gym, Not a Food Chain

But let's not forget about the rest of the ecosystem. The investors, mentors, incubators, and accelerators. They're the scaffolding that supports the crazy, chaotic construction site of the startup world. They provide the funds, the advice, the networks, and the emotional support (usually in the form of motivational quotes and free pizza). They're the unsung heroes of the startup ecosystem's resilience.

Resilience: The Secret Sauce of Startup Success

So, what's the secret sauce that makes the startup ecosystem so resilient? It's a combination of relentless innovation, fearless adaptation, and a healthy dose of stubborn optimism. It's the ability to turn failures into lessons, challenges into opportunities, and a garage into a multi-billion dollar empire. It's the shared belief that, no matter what the world throws at them, startups will keep on surviving, thriving, and driving the future.

In conclusion, the resilience of the startup ecosystem is nothing short of remarkable. It's a testament to the power of innovation, the courage of entrepreneurs, and the support of a community. So, whether you're a seasoned startup veteran, a fresh-faced founder, or an innocent bystander, take a moment to appreciate the cockroach-like resilience of the startup ecosystem. Because, let's face it, in a world full of uncertainties, it's comforting to know that startups, just like cockroaches, are here to stay.

6.2. Preparing for the Unknown: The Future of Startups, or How to Be a Startup Psychic Without a Crystal Ball

AH, THE FUTURE. THAT vast, unfathomable expanse of uncertainty that keeps entrepreneurs up at night. It's like trying to read a book in a language you don't understand, in the dark, with one eye closed. But fear not, dear reader, because preparing for the unknown doesn't require a crystal ball or a time machine. Just a healthy dose of startup chutzpah, a pinch of foresight, and maybe a stiff drink. So, let's dive into the murky waters of the future, shall we?

Forecasting: A Startup Weather Report

Firstly, let's talk about forecasting. Now, I'm not talking about predicting the weather (though that could come in handy when planning your next team-building beach trip). I'm talking about making educated guesses about market trends, customer needs, and competitive landscapes. It's like trying to predict what your teenager will want for dinner next week - impossible, frustrating, but oddly satisfying when you get it right.

Adaptation: The Startup Chameleon

Next, let's tackle adaptation. In the world of startups, the only constant is change. And I mean, constant. Like, "why are we pivoting again, didn't we just pivot last week?" constant. The key to surviving this whirlwind of change is to be adaptable. Be ready to pivot, iterate, and reiterate until you're dizzy. Because in the startup world, the stubborn don't survive, they just get left behind.

Innovation: The Startup Secret Weapon

Lastly, let's not forget about innovation. It's the secret weapon of every successful startup. It's what separates the unicorns from the donkeys, the Apples from the lemons. It's about thinking outside the box, even if that box is a cramped garage or a tiny co-working space cubicle. So, keep innovating, keep disrupting, and keep surprising everyone, including yourself.

The Unknown: Your Startup Adventure

In conclusion, preparing for the unknown is part and parcel of the startup journey. It's like embarking on an adventure with no map, no compass, and no clue what's waiting around the next corner. But with the right mindset, the right tools, and the right attitude, you can navigate the future with confidence, resilience, and a dash of startup swagger.

So, strap in, hold on, and enjoy the ride. Because the future of startups is unknown, unpredictable, and unbelievably exciting. And remember, as a wise man (or was it a fortune cookie?) once said, "The best way to predict the future is to create it". So, go out there and create your future, one startup at a time.

The maybe : Success

Ah, the startup success story. It's the stuff of legend, the gleaming pot of gold at the end of a caffeine-fueled, sleep-deprived, instant-ramen rainbow. When everything goes just right, when the planets align and the startup gods smile upon you, the rewards are nothing short of spectacular.

Let's paint a picture, shall we?

Firstly, there's the money. Boatloads of it. The kind of wealth that makes Scrooge McDuck's money bin look like a piggy bank. You'll have so much cash that you won't know what to do with it. Buy a private island? Why not two? Fund a mission to Mars? Elon, eat your heart out.

Then there's the fame. Suddenly, you're a rockstar of the business world. Your face graces the cover of Forbes. You're giving TED talks. You become a household name, and your startup jargon becomes the new lingua franca. Move over, Shakespeare. There's a new bard in town.

And who can forget the power? With a successful startup, you become a veritable king or queen. You have the power to change industries, influence markets, and shape the future. You can disrupt or create, build or destroy. It's like playing god, but with more press releases and less smiting.

But here's the best part: the satisfaction. There's nothing quite like the feeling of seeing your brainchild grow and flourish, of knowing that you brought something new into the world and made it work against all odds. It's the feeling of victory, of triumph, of standing on top of the world and shouting, "I did it!"

But let's be real. This is the Grumpy Entrepreneur talking. Remember, for every Instagram, there's a thousand startups that didn't make it. So, don't get your hopes up too high. And always remember to enjoy the journey, because the destination is far from guaranteed.

About the Author

David Murray-Hundley, fondly known as "The Grumpy Entrepreneur," is a remarkably distinguished figure in the world of entrepreneurship and business. Renowned for his straight-talking, no-nonsense attitude, and an unshakeable resolve, he has created a reputation that reflects both his business acumen and his unique persona.

Born in the United Kingdom, Murray-Hundley began his career in the technology sector, where he quickly made his mark. His first venture was Commerce One, a successful tech startup that he co-founded in the late 90s. Despite its initial success, the company was a casualty of the dot com crash, which served as a pivotal learning experience for Murray-Hundley.

Read more at https://www.parioventures.com.

About the Publisher